T0065106

CONFIRMING JUSTICE—
Or
INJUSTICE?

Also by Alan Dershowitz

CONFIRMING JUSTICE—
Or
INJUSTICE?

*A Guide to
Judging RBG's Successor*

ALAN
DERSHOWITZ

HOT BOOKS

Hot Books may be purchased in bulk at special discounts for sales promotion, corporate gifts, fund-raising, or educational purposes. Special editions can also be created to specifications. For details, contact the Special Sales Department, Skyhorse Publishing, 307 West 36th Street, 11th Floor, New York, NY 10018 or info@skyhorsepublishing.com.

Hot Books® and Skyhorse Publishing® are registered trademarks of Skyhorse Publishing, Inc.®, a Delaware corporation.

Visit our website at www.hotbookspress.com.

10 9 8 7 6 5 4 3 2 1

Library of Congress Cataloging-in-Publication Data is available on file.

ISBN: 978-1-5107-6567-2
eBook: 978-1-5107-6568-9

Cover design by Brian Peterson

Printed in the United States of America

*This book is dedicated to the few public figures
who place principle over partisanship.*

TABLE OF CONTENTS

Introduction

President Trump's nomination of Judge Amy Coney Barrett just weeks before the presidential election will create yet another confirmation battle along partisan lines. Judge Barrett is a highly qualified appellate-court judge, favored by religious conservatives and others on the right, whose rushed nomination and consideration by the Republican-controlled Senate is seen by Democrats as unfair in light of its refusal to consider President Obama's nomination of an equally qualified candidate much earlier in the 2016 election year. Her appointment, as the ninth and potentially swing vote, is seen as endangering a woman's right to choose, Obamacare, immigration, voting rights, and other agenda items important to Democrats. Her relative youth—she is forty-eight years old—was a factor in her selection by a president who said he was seeking a justice who could serve for "fifty years." All these elements combine to make her confirmation process one of the most contentious and important in recent history.

The process of nominating and confirming a Supreme Court justice has become among the most divisive activities in contemporary politics. It wasn't supposed to be that way, according to the Framers of our Constitution. And it didn't become the "blood sport" we are now witnessing until relatively recent times. But over the past several decades, the rules and traditions for nominating and confirming justices have been changed by the party in power—both Democrats and Republicans—to serve their short-term electoral and long-term ideological interests with little concern for the legitimacy, integrity, and credibility of the Supreme Court or the welfare of the nation as a whole.

The Framers had in mind a Supreme Court that in Hamilton's words would be "the least dangerous" branch, with neither sword nor purse—only respect and integrity to enforce its judgments. Its justices would be nominated by the president, with the advice and consent of the senate, which was to be comprised of distinguished elders selected not by popular vote but by state legislatures. Sage advice of these wise men would be sought by the president before he selected the justice and before they gave their consent to the nomination. The role of the High Court would be modest: to apply the Constitution and federal law and to resolve conflicts between the other two branches. But as the High Court has decided more controversial cases that impact many Americans, the public—and hence the politicians—have taken a greater interest in who becomes a justice and how they are chosen. In one sense, this has increased the democratization of the selection process, but in another sense, it has increased the politization of that process. The two go hand in hand.

There is a direct correlation, not only in this country but in other democracies, between the activism of the justices in matters directly affecting the public—such as abortion, gay rights, desegregation, prayer in schools, and other agenda issues—and the politization of the selection process. Put more simply, when a court tends to limit its decisions to narrow, technical matters that have little impact on voters, no one (except law professors and lawyers) really cares who gets appointed. But when courts begin to influence the daily lives of voters, these voters, quite understandably, want to have input into who is affecting their lives. This is not intended as a criticism or defense of judicial activism. I have written about those issues elsewhere.[1] It is an empirical observation based on historical evidence.

Until the twentieth century, the Supreme Court rendered relatively few decisions on issues of great concern to voters. Many, if not most, decisions were unanimous, or near unanimous. *Dred Scott*—the 1857 decision that declared that the descendants of enslaved people are not included among citizens entitled to legal rights—was a striking exception,[2] and it led to the Civil War. There were some other important decisions that influenced the daily lives of voters, but they were few and far between, at least as compared to those rendered by the current Supreme Court. Not

---

1   Dershowitz, *Shouting Fire*, Little Brown (2002).

2   Even that outrageously immoral decision was based on somewhat narrow technical reasoning, with little express attention paid to the larger issues of policy or morality.

surprisingly, therefore, there were some, but not many, contested nominations or partisan votes. Nominees were not questioned by committees and many were confirmed by unanimous voice votes.

Even as late as the early 1930s, bipartisan consensus nominations were common, as illustrated by the following account of how the seat opened by the resignation of the great Justice Oliver Wendell Holmes was filled by President Herbert Hoover.

Hoover, a Republican, nominated Cardozo, a Democrat, to replace Oliver Wendell Holmes, Jr. who had retired at age 90. Although Cardozo was a Democrat, he had support from across the political spectrum. Cardozo had served for 18 years on the New York Court of Appeals, first as an associate judge then as Chief Judge and his reputation had grown nationwide. Cardozo had written several respected books including his 1921 classic *The Nature of the Judicial Process.*

Although the brilliant jurist had few critics, some felt that Hoover could have been more strategic in his nomination. Cardozo was from New York, and two other New Yorkers—Harlan Fiske Stone and Charles Evans Hughes—were already on the court. Justice Louis Brandeis, the first Jewish justice, was still on the court.

Yet, Cardozo had two powerful Republican senators on his side. William Borah of Idaho, chairman of the Foreign Relations Committee, and George Norris of Nebraska.

Hoover talked to Borah the day before his announcement. The President showed Borah a list of potential nominees in descending order of Hoover's preference . . . Borah glanced at it, and believing Cardozo should be at the top, told Hoover, "Your list is alright, but you handed it to me upside down."

Borah reportedly told Hoover, "Cardozo belongs as much to Idaho as to New York," and "geography should no more bar the judge than the presence of two Virginians . . . should have kept President Adams from naming John Marshall to be Chief Justice."

As for Cardozo's being a Jew, Borah reportedly told Hoover, "Anyone who raises the question of race is unfit to advise you concerning so important a matter."

The Senate Judiciary Committee unanimously approved Cardozo's nomination on February 20, and the full Senate unanimously confirmed his nomination by voice vote, without debate or roll call, four days later.[3]

We have come a long way from those days of bipartisan nomination and confirmation of the most highly qualified jurists to serve on our nation's highest court. Today the criteria are rarely neutral assessments of judicial qualifications, but rather party affiliation, political ideology, gender and ethnic identity, and youth (so they can serve long terms).

It would be unthinkable today for a conservative Republican president to nominate a liberal Democrat. The party and the base would never stand for it. They demand the appointment of one of their own. The younger and more ideologically committed, the better. Today, Justices Ginsburg, Holmes, Brandeis and other great jurists would be excluded from consideration because they were sixty years old when nominated, though they all served long terms on the High Court.

Moreover, presidents do not want to repeat "the

---

3   Chicago-Kent College of Law, "SCOTUS Now" by Bridget Flynn and Christopher Schmidt, Feb. 15, 2019.

Souter mistake"—or what is now coming to be referred to as "The Roberts Mistake." Justice David Souter, a moderate Republican, was nominated by Republican President George H.W. Bush. He turned out to be far *too* centrist for many Republicans. Chief Justice John Roberts was appointed by Republican President George W. Bush. Although he continues to vote frequently with the other four Republican justices, he has joined the Democratic appointees in casting the deciding vote on several agenda issues, much to the chagrin of many hardline Republicans.[4] (Roberts insists that there are no Republican or Democrat judges, but the 5-4 decision in *Bush v. Gore* makes it clear that this is an aspiration rather than a reality.)

So now presidents seek greater assurances—in the opinions, writings and speeches of potential nominees—that they will not disappoint by moving toward the middle.

The confirmation battle over Supreme Court justices—and, to a lesser extent, other federal judges— has become a pure power struggle in which principle

---

4   President Theodore Roosevelt reportedly said that his nomination of Oliver Wendell Holmes was a mistake, as did President Dwight Eisenhower, who called his nomination of Earl Warren "the biggest damn fool mistake I ever made."

and precedent take a back seat. I'm reminded of my grandmother, an immigrant from a shtetl in Poland where Jews were always being victimized. She saw the world, even the new world that she loved, through the prism of her shtetl experience. Every news story—from the death of President Roosevelt, to the Korean War, to a victory by the Brooklyn Dodgers, was assessed by asking the same question: "Was it good or bad for the Jews?" That was her frame of reference. Today, too many politicians have an equally narrow focus: is it good or bad for my party, for my election, and for my ideology? Not for the Supreme Court or the country!

How did we get to the troubling place we are now at when it comes to filling Supreme Court vacancies? Can we ever return to a place where justices are nominated and confirmed in a more reasonable and dignified manner? Is it possible to adopt neutral rules equally applicable to nominees of both parties? These are among the questions I will address in this short book.

How did we get here?

There is both a long and short answer to this question. The longer version requires a bit of history. The shorter version focuses on current events.

From the founding of our nation, there has been controversy regarding the role of judges. The Constitution created the judiciary as a coequal branch—at least in theory—along with the executive and legislative. The Federalists—led by Alexander Hamilton—saw the judiciary as a necessary check on the popular branches, while the Democratic Republicans—led by Thomas Jefferson—distrusted the appointed elite judiciary. But even Hamilton saw the judicial branch as extremely limited in its power, and especially in its ability to enforce its judgments. In *Federalist 78*, he discussed the "natural feebleness of the judiciary," characterizing it as "the weakest of the three departments of power," because it has "neither force nor will, but merely judgment; and must ultimately depend open the aid of the executive arm even for the efficacy of its judgments." This view proved to be prescient when President Andrew Jackson famously (or infamously) refused to enforce the judgment of the High Court in an important case involving the rights of native Americans. He was quoted—perhaps apocryphally—as saying: "John Marshall made his decision; now let him enforce it." Whether apocryphal or actual, the quote accurately reflects Jackson's view: the decision was never enforced.

Hamilton did argue that the federal courts necessarily have the power to strike down unconstitutional legislation and executive actions—which Chief Justice Marshall subsequently confirmed in the Court's decisions. But despite this important power, Hamilton still insisted that "though individual oppression may now and then proceed from the courts of justice, the general liberty of the people can never be endangered from that quarter. . . ."

Tragically, history has proved him only partly correct. There have been decisions that endangered the rights of African Americans, Japanese-Americans, women, gays, criminal defendants, mentally challenged individuals, political dissidents, and others. Many of these have taken the form of upholding legislative and executive actions, as Hamilton anticipated when he warned that "liberty can have nothing to fear from the judiciary alone, but would have everything to fear from its union with either of the other departments." Fortunately, many of the judicial decisions that have endangered segments of our population have been reversed over time, but courts still have the ability, especially if they become the enablers of the other branches, to endanger liberty.

Despite Hamilton's view regarding the limitations

on the power of the judiciary, presidents since John Adams have tried hard to assure that their political and ideological soulmates are appointed to the courts. On his way out of office, Adams nominated John Marshall, a Federalist, to become Chief Justice. He also nominated numerous "midnight judges," so named because he worked through the night signing their commissions before his term ended.

President Andrew Jackson sought to democratize the judiciary, as well as the country in general. Before Jackson, the word democracy was controversial. We were a republic with democratic elements, such as the House of Representatives. But the presidency and the senate were not popularly elected. And, certainly, judges were not subject to election, but Jacksonian democracy introduced the concept of elected judges in many states. Because of the constitution, the United States government maintained its tradition of appointed judges serving during good behavior.

For the next century or so, the process of nominating justices to the United States Supreme Court remained relatively uncontroversial. To be sure, there were some controversial choices during the run up to the Civil War and in the postwar period. President

Woodrow Wilson's nomination of Louis Brandeis in 1916 generated enormous controversy, because of his Jewish heritage. But eventually he, too, was confirmed and served with distinction for many years.

During the New Deal, the process of nominating justices again became front-page news as President Roosevelt proposed packing the court with additional justices for every sitting justice who reached a certain age. This tactic was designed to reduce the influence of "the nine old men," a majority of whom were routinely striking down New Deal legislation. After he made his threat to pack the court, several justices appeared more sympathetic to aspects of the New Deal, thus resulting in what pundits called "the switch in time that saved nine."

Between the New Deal and 1987 (when Robert Bork was nominated), there were only a few contentious nominations and confrontation battles, especially during the Nixon administration. In the fall of 1971, the Supreme Court had two vacancies resulting from the retirements of Justices Hugo Black and John Harlan. Having already appointed a new chief justice and one associate justice, President Richard Nixon had the opportunity to reshape the high court.

His first two attempts to fill these associate justice positions—Judges Clement Haynsworth and G. Harold Carswell—failed. Much controversy ensued.

At that time, I was a regular contributor to *The New York Times* Week in Review section, and I penned an article about the nomination process that made the following points, which remain all too relevant today. I began with a discussion of what the Senate may properly consider in evaluating a Supreme Court nominee.

Views about what a senator may and may not properly take into account vary. Charles Black, professor of constitutional law at Yale and a leading scholar of the Supreme Court, takes what is perhaps the most expansive view of the Senate's role: "There is just no reason at all for a Senator's not voting, in regard to confirmation of a Supreme Court nominee, on the basis of a full and unrestricted view, unencumbered by any presumption of the nominee's fitness for the office." Others take an extremely restrictive view of the Senate's proper role: according to them, a powerful presumption operates in favor of the president's choice, a presumption that may be overcome only in firm instances of demonstrated incompetence or corruption.

Standing between these poles is a continuum of views about the considerations—political, judicial, philosophical, and regional—that may properly be weighted by the Senate in exercising its constitutional duties to join with the president in appointing justices of the Supreme Court.

The words of the Constitution and the history of its adoption seem to support a position closer to the expansive view advocated by Professor Black than to the restrictive view that had held sway in the Senate during most of the twentieth century. Article 2 of the Constitution says that the president "shall nominate and by and with the advice and consent of the Senate, shall appoint . . . judges of the Supreme Court." The original proposal—which received considerable support at the Constitutional Convention—was for the Senate alone to appoint justices. Ultimately, a compromise was unanimously reached whereby the appointing function was divided between the president and the Senate. The Federalist Papers make it clear that the

Senate is supposed to take its "advice"-giving function seriously, in order to prevent the president from making undistinguished appointments—not merely incompetent or corrupt ones: "He would be both ashamed and afraid to bring forward candidates who had no other merit than that of coming from the same state . . . or being in some way or other personally allied to him, or of possessing the necessary insignificance and pliancy to render them the obsequious instruments of his pleasure."

I pointed out the important distinction between the Senate's role in confirming a nominee for the Supreme Court and one for a cabinet, or other executive, position:

The president should be given great latitude in picking his cabinet—the people who will be working with him and for him. Being "personally allied" to the president may well be a distance qualification for a cabinet post. But Supreme Court justices are not supposed to be the president's men [or women]; they are supposed to work neither with him nor for him. They should be as independent of him as they are of the Senate.

I then discussed the history of how the senate dealt with earlier nominations:

> As an early commentator put it: "A party nomination may be justly met by party opposition." Stated more generally, if a president nominates a justice on the basis of factors other than judicial excellence—factors such as party, region, or political views—then, the argument goes, the Senate is entitled to prefer its own party, region, or political views to those of the president. The Federalist Papers support the conclusion that the Senate need not sit back and allow a president to reap partisan political advantage from an appointment to the Supreme Court: "It would be an excellent check upon the spirit of favoritism in the President, and would tend greatly to prevent the appointment of unfit characters . . . from a view to popularity." Thus, if a president is entitled to try to implement a "Southern strategy," then the Senate is held to be equally entitled to try to frustrate it.
>
> Under this view, then, it is the president who decides the rules of the game: If he submits a nomination that is regionally motivated, the Senate may properly reject it on regional grounds; if he

submits a nomination to achieve certain political objective, then the Senate may properly reject it if it does not share these objectives. But if the president submits the name of a man or woman of real distinction or potential judicial greatness, then it would be improper for the Senate to attempt to convert the nomination into a political issue.

I then discussed the ideological views of the nominee:

The truly perplexing issue arises in the contest of a nominee who lacks sympathy with the value reflected in the Bill of Rights—who believes in "order" more than "justice," "security" more than "liberty," and "efficiency" more than "equality." Clemton Haynsworth and G. Harrold Carswell were both denied confirmation—at least in part— because of their reputed views on racial issues (as were a number of nominees during the pre-and post-Civil War eras). And a compelling case can be made for a senator's voting against an otherwise qualified nominee with a record demonstrating callousness about—or opposition to—civil rights or civil liberties.

The executive and legislative branches are adequate protectors of order, security, and efficiency. But here must be a coequal branch that is committed to the far more subtle—and far less popular—values of justice, liberty, and equality. That branch is the Supreme Court, and if its members—or a majority of them—were simply to mirror the value of the popular branches, then the uniqueness of the Court would be at an end. Under our constitutional system of government, it is as much the responsibility of the Supreme court as of the president to make certain that this does not happen.

Finally, I discussed the concept of judicial philosophy and its relevance to the senate confirmation process:

A judicial philosophy deals with the rules of the Court as an instrument. It is responsive to question such as: What precedential weight should be given to prior decisions? What power should the Court exercise over the other branches of the federal government and over the states? What tools of judicial construction should it employ in giving meaning to a constitutional or statutory provision? A judicial philosophy—if it is truly judicial rather than "political" or "social"—does not speak in terms of giving the peace forces "tools" to "protect the innocent from criminal elements."

A "conservative" judicial philosophy is one that respects precedent and avoids deciding cases on constitutional grounds whenever a narrower ground for a decision is available. Most important, a judge with a conservative judicial philosophy adjures employing the courts to effectuate his own political or social program—he is a decider of cases rather than an advocate of causes.

Justice Oliver Wendell Holmes descried such a judge as one who has "no thought but that of which he is bound," and who has learned "to solve a problem according to the rules by transcending [his or her] own convictions and to leave room for much that he would hold dear to be done away with.' In short, he or she is a judge who focuses concern on process rather than results, and who lets the political chips fall where they may.

This is why it is so difficult to predict how a true judicial conservative will decide a given issue. For him [or her], so much depends on how the issue is framed: on what the statute says, on the prior cases, on whether it arose in a federal or state context.

Justice Louis Brandeis was a judicial conservative, though a political liberal. Justice Holmes was a judicial and political conservative. But the judicial opinions of these giants tell us little about their individual political (or economic or social) views: for that, we must go to their extrajudicial writings. Indeed, many people are surprised to learn how differently these men felt about the social and political issues of their day, since their judicial opinions were so similar.

In the end, President Nixon nominated William Rehnquist and Lewis Powell. Both were confirmed and served with distinction, with Rehnquist later being promoted to Chief Justice.

The nomination of Judge Robert Bork to the Supreme Court, by President Ronald Regan in 1987, brought forth the fury of the Democratic party. Senator Ted Kennedy, with whom I closely worked on human rights and civil rights, made the following comment about Bork:

> Robert Bork's America is a land in which women would be forced into back-alley abortions, Blacks would sit at segregated lunch counters, rogue police

could break down citizens' doors in midnight raids, and schoolchildren could not be taught about evolution, writers and artists could be censored at the whim of the Government, and the doors of the Federal courts would be shut on the fingers of millions of citizens.

Ultimately, after a contentious set of hearings in which Bork did not present himself well, the nomination was narrowly defeated by a vote of 48-52. This led to Judge Bork's name becoming a verb, as in "to be borked," or "to bork" a nominee. The Republicans swore revenge, and eventually took it.

In 2013, after the Republicans blocked several lower court nominations, the Democrats changed the filibuster and cloture rules for all judicial nominees except Supreme Court justices. Prior to the change, a minority of forty senators could block a nomination, thus incentivizing presidents to nominate judges who would receive at least some support from the other party. With the change, a nominee—other than a justice—could be confirmed along party lines with a simple majority.

Then, in 2017, the Republicans deployed the so called "nuclear option" to prevent a filibuster of the nomination of Neil Gorsuch as a Supreme Court Justice. The Democrats were trying to block the Gorsuch nomination because they felt that the seat had been stolen from them by the unwillingness of the Republicans to allow President Obama's nomination of Judge Merrick Garland to come to a vote. Obama had nominated Garland eight months before the 2016 presidential election, immediately following the death of Justice Antonin Scalia. Republican leaders had insisted that no Supreme Court nomination should be considered in an election year. Here is what majority leader Mitch McConnell said: "The American people should have a voice in the selection of their next Supreme Court Justice. Therefore, this vacancy should not be filled until we have a new president." Judiciary Chairman Lindsey Graham was even more forceful in his opposition. "I want you to use my words against me. If there's a Republican president in 2016 and a vacancy occurs in the last year of the first term, you can say, 'Lindsey Graham said let's let the next president, whoever it might be, make that nomination.'"

When Graham's hypothetical became a reality in 2020 with the death of Justice Ruth Bader Ginsburg, both McConnell and Graham changed their tune. This is what McConnell said:

> Our Senate majority will do exactly the same thing
> in 2020 that we did in 2016: Follow Senate his-
> tory, follow the clear precedent in each situation,
> and do exactly the job we were elected to do. We
> are going to vote on President Trump's nominee to
> the Supreme Court this year."

And when Graham's words were used against him, this is how he tried to distinguish the two nominations:

> "Well, Merrick Garland was a different situation.
> You had the president of one party nominating, and
> you had the Senate in the hands of the other par-
> ty. A situation where you've got them both would
> be different. I don't want to speculate, but I think
> appointing judges is a high priority for me in 2020.

Any lawyer worth his salt can draw distinctions between cases and argue that the earlier case is not a
precedent for the current one. But a distinction without a difference is not persuasive. Moreover, Senator
Graham did not say in 2016 that his precedent was
limited to situations where the presidency and senate were controlled by different parties. Eventually,
Graham argued that he had changed his mind because

of the way Brett Kavanaugh was treated by the Democrats. "After Kavanaugh, the rules have changes, as far as I'm concerned." Graham was referring to the hotly disputed allegations of sexual misconduct when Kavanaugh was in high school that took center stage at the Kavanaugh hearings.

Senator Ted Cruz was more candid when he said that the Democrats would be doing the same thing:

"If the president were Joe Biden or Hillary Clinton and Chuck Schumer were the majority leader, the odds are 100 percent" that Democrats would seek to nominate and confirm a replacement for Ruth Bader Ginsburg as soon as possible. Senator John Barrasso argued that, "If the shoe were on the other foot and the Democrats had the White House and the Senate, they would right now be trying to confirm another member of the Supreme Court."

I'm sure they are right about that. But hypocrisy by one party doesn't justify it by the other party. Two Republican Senators, Susan Collins of Maine and Lisa Murkowski of Alaska, have announced that they will remain consistent with what the Republicans did in 2016 and refuse to vote to confirm a nominee so late in the election cycle.

Moreover, the Democrats have a somewhat more

persuasive distinction between 2016 and now. In 2016, the nomination was made eight months, not five weeks, before the election. But I have no doubt that if the timing were reversed, the leaders of both parties would subordinate principle, precedent, and consistency to my grandmother's criteria: is it good or bad for my party?

We are now in a situation in which principles, precedents, and consistency are trumped by raw power. President Trump put it this way: "When you have the Senate, when you have the votes, you can sort of do what you want. . . ." Both parties will do whatever they have the votes to do, regardless of what they have said or done in the past, or what they plan to do in the future. Jefferson's "Manual of Parliamentary Practice of the Use of the Senate of the United States" has been replaced by Machiavelli's advice to authoritarian leaders and Sun Tzu's prescription for fighting wars.

Both parties not only fail the shoe-on-the-other-foot test, they actually invoke that moral test as a weapon against its applicability. They point out— quite accurately—that if the shoe were on the other foot, the opposing party would do exactly what they are accused of doing. They fight fire with fire, arguing that their hypocrisy is justified by the other side's hypocrisy. It's childish—"he started it"—but it seems to work with most senators and many voters in the base. If it continues to work—if there is no push back against partisan hypocrisy—it will only get worse. I'm reminded of FDR's response to a critic who accused him of supporting a Central American dictator: "Yes, he's an SOB, but he's OUR SOB." Today, party loyalists are saying about their leaders: "He's an unprincipled hypocrite, but he's OUR unprincipled hypocrite."

Although the immediate stimulus for this was the death of Justice Ginsburg and the nomination of Judge Barrett to replace her, the important issues raised by this singular event transcend today's headlines. They will be with us for years to come unless there are institutional changes in the way we select our justices.

The question remains: can we get ourselves out of this deepening quagmire and save the Supreme Court from becoming yet another casualty of our growing hyper-partisan descent into unprincipled hypocrisy? I will address this question, among others, in the coming chapters, and will propose solutions in the conclusion.[5]

---

5   As soon as Justice Ginsburg's death was announced, I began to write a series of op-eds regarding the process for replacing her. Much of what follows in Chapters 1-7 is adapted from these op-eds.

CHAPTER 1

The Role of the President in Nominating a Justice: Does President Trump Have the Power to Nominate RBG's Replacement?

The unexpected death of Justice Ruth Bader Ginsburg set off a great debate that could affect the future of not only the Supreme Court but of the nation as a whole. Should the President have nominated a justice to replace Justice Ruth Bader Ginsburg just six weeks before the presidential election? Now that he has, should the Senate act on the nomination? Or should it refuse to, as it did when President Obama nominated Merrick Garland eight months before the election?

In considering these issues, it is crucial to distinguish between the *constitutional powers* of the president and senate on the one hand, and political considerations on the other hand. As my colleague, Professor Laurence Tribe, put it: "I'm not suggesting its unconstitutional to go ahead, it's perfectly constitutional. But a lot of things that are constitutional are stupid."

So let's analyze both the constitutionality and wisdom—or lack thereof—of the current rush to nominate and confirm Judge Barrett. We begin with the constitutional powers. There is absolutely no doubt that the Constitution permits a president to nominate justices until the last hours of his term in office. If an outgoing president were to nominate a justice on the morning of January 20th, just hours before his term was over, that nomination would be constitutionally valid. We know that not only from the text of the constitution, but from precedent. President John Adams nominated John Marshall to be Chief Justice just before he turned the office over to Thomas Jefferson. President Herbert Hoover nominated Benjamin Cardozo just weeks before he turned the presidency over to Franklin Delano Roosevelt. President Jimmy Carter nominated Stephen Breyer to the Court of Appeals after he was defeated for reelection by Ronald Reagan. In these and other cases, the senate confirmed the nominations, and the nominees went on to serve long and distinguished terms. There are other instances as well of nominations in the shadow of an election.

So the constitutional and legal powers of the president and senate are clear beyond dispute. But just because the president and senate have this power does not necessarily mean they should exercise it. Persuasive arguments have been made on both sides of this issue. When President Obama nominated Merrick Garland, Senate Majority Leader Mitch McConnell and Judiciary Committee Chairman Lindsey Graham, along with other Republican senators, insisted that it was wrong for a president to nominate and for the Senate to confirm a Supreme Court nominee during a presidential election year. But now that the shoe is in the other foot, McConnell and other Republican senators, including Graham, have made arguments seeking to distinguish President Obama's nomination of Garland from President Trump's nomination of Judge Amy Coney Barrett. They argue that the situation is different when the president and the senate are from the same party, as they are now, than when the president is from one party and the senate is controlled by the other party, as was the case with

Obama's nomination of Garland. This is a political issue that the voters will have to assess in the coming election, in which both McConnell and Graham are in close races. Voters will have to decide whether these senators have violated principles that they themselves articulated when it benefited their party. For many senators on both sides of the aisle, partisanship will prevail over principle, as it generally does when the political stakes are high.

It is not only Republican senators who have changed views they expressed in 2016: Democratic senators have done so as well, including Senate Minority Leader Chuck Schumer. Even presidential candidate Joe Biden has flip-flopped on this issue: back in 1992, he opposed President George H.W. Bush nominating a justice before the election, but then in 2016, he supported President Obama nominating Merrick Garland, and now is opposed to President Trump nominating a replacement for Justice Ginsburg.

One argument that is being made today by Republican Senators, and was made by Democrats back in 2016, is that it is dangerous to have eight justices on the Supreme Court without a ninth justice to break ties. When that argument was offered by Democrats in 2016, Republicans responded by arguing that a Supreme Court with eight justices can operate effectively, since relatively few decisions are decided on 5-4 votes. Today, some Republicans are arguing that it is especially important that a ninth justice be appointed because of the likelihood that the 2020 presidential election may well end up in the Supreme Court, as did the 2000 election. In *Bush v. Gore*, the Supreme Court decided by a 5-4 majority along strictly party lines to stop the Florida recount, which effectively gave the election to the Republican candidate George W. Bush.

So the question arises: What would be worse for America—a 4-4 tie in the Supreme Court which let the lower court ruling stand; or a 5-4 decision in which the deciding vote was cast by a justice nominated on the eve of the election by a president who is a litigant in the case before the justices?

There is, of course, a third alternative. Chief Justice John Roberts is a master at avoiding Supreme Court decisions that appear to be partisan in nature. He is determined to keep the high court above politics. And he has the skills to persuade justices to do what is best for the Supreme Court as an institution. Whether he will be able to do this in the current highly divisive political climate is uncertain.

Already two Republican senators have said they will not vote to confirm a justice nominated on the eve of the election. Two more defectors would be necessary to stop the confirmation. Whether any other Republican senators will join the two may well depend on how the nominee does at the hearings.

CHAPTER 2

The Role of the Senate: Placing Principle above Partisanship in Replacing Justice Ginsburg

When I presented the constitutional arguments on the Senate floor against the impeachment and removal of President Trump, several Republican senators praised me for placing principle over partisanship. I am a liberal democrat who voted for Hilary Clinton, but I strongly believed that the Constitutional criteria for impeaching President Trump had not been satisfied by the House of Representatives. So, placing Constitutional principles above party loyalty, I incurred the wrath of many Democrats and friends by opposing the impeachment and removal of President Trump.

Now I urge the Republican Senators who praised me for placing principle above partisanship to do the same when it comes to replacing the late, great Justice Ruth Bader Ginsburg. Although the Constitution is silent on the timing of nominating and confirming a justice on the eve of a presidential election, Republican senators were anything but silent when former President Barack Obama nominated the highly qualified Judge Merritt Garland eight months before the 2016 presidential election. They insisted that no Supreme Court nomination be confirmed during a presidential election year.

These and other senators are now demanding the hasty nomination and confirmation process on the eve of the 2020 presidential election. In doing so, they are placing partisanship above principles—their own stated principles. This is not to say that some Democratic senators would not do the same thing if the shoe were on the other foot. During the Garland confirmation process, numerous Democratic senators insisted that it was entirely proper to confirm the nomination of a justice more than two-thirds of a year before a presidential election. They will surely argue that there is a difference, if only in degree, based on proximity to the election. Joe Biden has also flip-flopped on this issue, as have many partisan "experts," commentators, and ordinary citizens.

But just as two wrongs do not make a right, hypocrisy on both sides of the aisle does not make it principled.

The principle—articulated by both parties when it served their interests—is to defer the nomination of a potential swing justice until the president—whether newly elected or reelected—is sworn in on January 20, 2021. This allows voters to decide which candidate they trust more to make this important nomination. Though, in theory, nominations to the Supreme Court should never be partisan, the reality is that presidents campaign on the promise to nominate justices who promote their agenda. Indeed, President Trump has a published list of conservative judges, lawyers, and politicians from which he will select his nominee. He has placed that issue before the voting public, and the voters should have an opportunity to decide whether he or his opponent—who has pledged to nominate a Black woman—should be entrusted with the important decision of who to nominate to the highest court at a time of considerable division among the justices.

Moreover, if Republican Senators act against the principles they articulated during the Garland confirmation, they risk further politicizing the Supreme Court in the event of a Democratic victory this November.

Those who are pushing to seat a new justice before the election point to the possibility of a 4–4 tie vote if he results of the election were to be challenged in the Highest Court, as they were in 2000. Those on the other side argue that a 5–4 vote decided by last minute pre-election nominee would be even worse than a tie vote. Neither would be good for credibility of the Supreme Court. Nor are the threats by some Democrats, who are promising to expand the number of Supreme Court justices if the Democrats were to win the presidency and the senate. President Franklin Delano Roosevelt tried that back in the 1930s when the Supreme Court undercut his New Deal, but public opinion strongly opposed such overt politicization of the high court and led the president to withdraw his ill-advised plan. Playing politics with the Supreme Court—whether by rushing a nomination through on the eve of the election or expanding the number of justices—would damage the integrity of the high court at a time when it is most needed.

The future of the Supreme Court may be at stake, and senators have a critical role to play in assuring that the process of selecting a justice is determined by enduring principles rather than immediate partisan advantage.

CHAPTER 3

The Role of the Sitting Justice: Should Ginsburg Have Retired While Barack Obama was President?

In the midst of all the well-deserved praise being accorded to the late Justice Ruth Bader Ginsburg, some Democrats are grumbling about her decision not to retire while Barack Obama was president and the Senate was controlled by Democrats. Had she done so, her replacement most certainly would have been a liberal woman who could have served on the' high court for decades. Ginsburg was in her mid-seventies at the time and had already suffered one bout of cancer. She was urged by friends to retire while President

Obama could pick her successor. But she made a decision not to, because she believed she had many good years left to serve and cast votes in important cases. She ended up serving with distinction for nearly an additional decade.

In explaining to friends and colleagues why she made the decision to remain on the court, she reportedly said that she had never allowed men to tell her what to do and she was not about to allow Democratic politicians and supporters, mostly men, to demand her resignation, while she still had her mental and physical acuity. And indeed she worked hard to maintain that acuity by exercising—even allowing a book to be written about her exercise regime by her trainer.

So the following question is now being asked: Did she put her own selfish interests ahead of those Democrats and liberals whose future may well be affected by her decision not to resign earlier?

Let there be no mistake that Ruth Bader Ginsburg, whom I knew for nearly half a century from her time as a professor and an ACLU lawyer, was a zealous liberal, and sometimes partisan. She made her negative views about President Trump public and clear, and she reportedly told her granddaughter that her dying wish was not to be replaced by a president who would obviously select someone whose views were the polar opposite of her own.

She wanted to have it both ways: she wanted to continue serving on the Supreme Court for as long as possible; and she hoped to retire or die when a Democratic president could name her successor. But as an old Yiddish expression goes: "Man (and woman) plan; God laughs." God obviously upset Ginsburg's plans by taking her on Rosh Hashanah eve—a time reserved in Jewish tradition for the death of only the most righteous. But death trumped Ginsburg's wishes, and President Trump got to name her successor, a judge who may try hard to reverse at least some decisions that Ginsburg supported.

So was she right or wrong in her decision not to retire earlier? I think she was right, but for reasons different from those currently offered in her defense. Those who urged her to time her resignation so as to secure a liberal replacement fail to take into account important institutional considerations. For the Supreme Court to retain its credibility as a non-partisan institution that serves as a check and balance against the elected branches of government, its members must not only be non-partisan, they must appear to be non-partisan. Justice must not only be done, but it must be *seen* to be done. Timing resignations to assure replacements in kind undercut the neutrality of the Supreme Court. Tragically, they reflect the current reality in which partisanship influences nomination and confirmation. For partisanship to also influence resignations and deaths would only further undercut the neutrality of the Supreme Court.

In response to my call for non-partisanship, many on both sides of the aisle will argue that the other side started it. And they are both right. It was then-Chairman of the Judiciary Committee, Joe Biden, who urged President George H.W. Bush not to nominate a justice in the run-up to the election. But when he was Vice President, Biden supported President Obama's nomination of Merrick Garland eight months before the 2016 election. Now he opposes President Trump's nomination just weeks before the 2020 election. On the other side of the aisle, we have Lindsey Graham, who in 2016 successfully opposed bringing the Garland nomination to the Senate, and now strongly supports bringing President Trump's nomination to that same body. And then we have Justice Ginsberg herself, who in 2016 stated that the President has the authority to nominate a justice as long as he serves in office.

Unfortunately, partisan politics will continue to influence the Supreme Court in many ways. This will only weaken it as an institution over the long run.

CHAPTER 4:

The Role of the Vice President: Can He Cast the Deciding Vote On Whether the Senate Consents to a Supreme Court Nominee?

Never in our history has a Supreme Court nomination been confirmed by an equally divided vote among the senators, with the Vice President breaking the tie. At the moment, only two Republican senators have said they will not vote to confirm President Trump's nominee, but if one additional Republican senator were to decide to vote no—perhaps based on Judge Barrett's answers to questions—we may be confronting that outcome. Did the Framers of our Constitution intend such a result? There are several provisions that cast light on this question of first impression.

The reason this is a question of first impression is that until recently, a Supreme Court nominee needed a supermajority under the rules and traditions of the Senate. So a tie vote defeated a nomination. Only now that a simple majority is enough does the question arise whether the Vice President can break a tie in the context of a Supreme Court nominee.

The three provisions of the Constitution that are most relevant are the following: Article 2 empowers the president to "nominate and by and with the advice and consent of the Senate, shall appoint ... Judges of the Supreme Court..."; Article 1 provides that "The Vice President shall be President of the Senate, but shall have no vote, unless they be equally divided;" Article 1 also states that "Each house may determine the rules of its proceedings."

It is clear therefore that in voting on proposed statutes, the Vice President is authorized to cast a tie breaking vote. Did the Framers intend the same rule to apply when the president is seeking the advice and consent of senators to a judicial nomination? We can't know for certain because the constitutional and Federalist Papers focused on the Vice

President's role in breaking ties over legislation, not confirmation. Is the advice and consent function of the senate different and more personal than its legislative function, thus requiring a majority of actual senators to consent to a judicial appointment? As a matter of good policy, should a justice be confirmed for a lifetime appointment without the consent of a majority of the actual senators? Would allowing the Vice President to break the tie give the White House undue power in the selection of a justice by having the President make the nomination and *his* Vice President cast the deciding vote to consent to it? (Recall that at the time of the Constitution, the Vice President was the runner-up candidate who lost to the president. The Twelfth Amendment changed that, making the Vice President the president's running mate.) Would it be proper for a senator who was on the fence to cast a negative vote in order to avoid a tie that would be broken by the Vice President?

These are serious questions that should be asked and answered by every senator—and every voter. Judge Amy Coney Barrett is forty-eight years old. If she lives as long as Justice Ginsberg, she could serve nearly forty years based on a confirmation by less than a majority of sitting senators.

In my view, the Framers made a mistake by not requiring a supermajority for the confirmation of a justice to a lifelong term. The requirement of a super-majority—whether two-thirds or three-fifths—would incentivize a president to nominate consensus candidates who require the votes of at least some senators from the opposing party. For decades, senators tried to remedy, or at least ameliorate, the effects of this mistake by internal rules requiring a supermajority. That safeguard was ended by partisan decisions (ending the filibuster and deploying the nuclear option) by both parties. So now, all that is required is a simple majority to confirm controversial and divisive Supreme Court nominees. But a tie vote broken by the Vice President would weaken even the requirement of a simple majority, thus encouraging presidents to nominate increasingly divisive justices.

Senators will now have to decide whether to go further down this road of divisiveness and politicization of the Supreme Court. They have several options: to go back to the requirement of a supermajority for Supreme Court nominees, to require an actual majority (i.e., fifty-one senators) to confirm a Supreme Court nominee, or to allow confirmation of a justice by a tie vote broken by the Vice President whose President made the nomination.

Now that President Trump has announced his pick, senators will have to decide on the merits of his nominee. They will also have to decide whether the refusal of the senate to consider President Obama's nomination of Judge Merrick Garland eight months before the 2016 election should serve as a precedent for how this nomination is treated. Finally, they may have to decide, in the event of a tie vote, whether to confirm a justice who has not secured the consent of a majority of sitting senators. These are daunting decisions that will impact our nation for generations.

CHAPTER 5

The Role of the Constitution: What If Justice Ginsburg Were In a Coma?

With no disrespect for the recently departed Justice Ruth Bader Ginsburg, as a law professor, I must explore the following hypothetical situation which could well have taken place with regard to her and might well take place with regard to a justice in the future. What would the situation be now if Justice Ginsburg had gone into a long coma, but remained alive through the end of the current Presidential term? We know what would happen if a president were to be comatose. The 25th amendment would kick in: a process would be in place for replacing him either temporarily or permanently. But there is no such constitutional amendment for a justice of the Supreme court. The Constitution provides that a justice may serve during good behavior. Being in a coma is not bad behavior. Nor is it an impeachable offence. A comatose justice would not have the mental capacity to resign. Nor under the constitution could she or he be compelled to resign while incapacitated.

When Justice Thurgood Marshall was ailing near the end of his life, he quipped to his law clerks: "If I die, prop me up and keep on voting." Justice Marshall, whom I knew for many years, had a great sense of humor, including about his own mortality. Justice Ginsburg left no such instructions, humorous or otherwise. She did reportedly tell her granddaughter that she did not want to be replaced by President Trump, but under the Constitution her dying wishes have no impact on who nominates her replacement and when it is made.

Throughout our history, we have had judges who have become incapacitated, through senility or other illnesses. One was diagnosed with "incurable lunacy" but did not retire. Seriously incapacitated justices and judges have generally retired through informal pressures by their colleagues. But, in the highly public and politicized process of replacing a justice, the legal procedures should be crystal clear to avoid partisan manipulation. They are not clear today. Nor could they necessarily be clarified by statute or regulation, as has been tried over the years. The words of the Constitution prevail, and they provide for life tenure during good behavior.

Some would argue that good behavior is an affirmative criteria and that a comatose justice could not engage in such behavior and so must be removed from the court and a replacement selected. But such a view would surely be contested in a situation like the one we now face, where a liberal Democrat is being replaced by a conservative Republican. If a president of the opposite party from the justice were to nominate a replacement in the absence of the resignation or death of the incumbent, there would surely be a loud outcry from the other side. Nor is it clear who would resolve any partisan dispute over the power of the president to replace a comatose justice. The president would claim such power. The Senate, if it were under the control of the President's party, might well confirm his nominee. The Supreme Court would have little choice but to seat the replacement justice. But the integrity of the court would be damaged and the legitimacy of the justice would be questioned.

To further exacerbate the situation and to make the hypothetical more interesting, what if the comatose justice were then to fully recover? Could she or he claim their seat, arguing that they did not relinquish it as a matter of law? These questions, though hypothetical, are what keep law professors and their students awake, if not at night, at least in the classroom.

Although normally I have opinions about such matters of constitutional law, I must admit I have no idea what would have happened if Justice Ginsburg had fallen into a coma and remained alive until January 20th, 2021. It didn't happen this time, but it could happen sooner rather than later, especially since several justices are now at an age at which strokes and other medical conditions are not beyond the realm of possibility.

So let's plan now for such an eventuality. A constitutional amendment, akin to the 25th, should be proposed for Supreme Court justices. Since we now don't know which justices, if any, might be affected by this situation, it may be possible to get a consensus regarding this matter. The great philosopher John Rawls wrote that the best way to secure justice is for those making the decisions not to know how it will impact them, or in this case their party. We now live in a Rawlsian world when it comes to a disabled justice, so it is the right time to plan for the future and establish a rule that will operate regardless of person, party, or ideology.

CHAPTER 6

The Role of the Judiciary Committee: What Questions May Senators Properly Ask Judge Barrett About Her Catholic Faith?

When Judge Amy Coney Barrett came before the Senate Judiciary Committee in 2017 for her nomination to the Court of Appeals, Senator Diane Feinstein generated considerable controversy when she said to Barrett, "The dogma lives loudly within you." This was a reference to Barrett's deep Catholic faith. Under our Constitution, Senator Feinstein's statement crossed the line. Ours was the first Constitution in history to provide that *"no religious test* shall ever be required as a Qualification to any Office or public Trust under the United States." Although Feinstein did not explicitly impose a religious test, she suggested that personal religious views—which she called dogma—might disqualify a nominee from being confirmed. That would clearly be unconstitutional.

When Justice Louis Brandeis was nominated to the United States Supreme Court in 1916, numerous leaders of the bar and prominent Americans, including the president of Harvard, opposed his nomination, sometimes implicitly, sometimes explicitly, on the ground that he was Jewish. That was wrong then, and it is equally wrong today with regard to a nominee of the Catholic faith.

Indeed, today's Supreme Court has five justices who are Catholic, two who are Jewish, and one who is Protestant. Religious tests have no place in America. But what does have a place in the confirmation process are questions about whether a nominee will put faith before the Constitution and refuse to apply the Constitution if it conflicts with his or her faith. That issue would be true of any nominee, regardless of their faith or faithlessness. President John Kennedy assured us that his Catholicism would not determine the nation's policy. Justice Scalia said the same about his Catholicism and his jurisprudence.

It is impossible, of course, to psychoanalyze a nominee or justice to determine what role, if any, their faith may play in their jurisprudence. We are all influenced by our personal views, including, but not limited to, religious views. When Justice Pierce Butler issued the sole dissent in the notorious case of *Buck v. Bell*—in which the Supreme Court led by Justice Oliver Wendell Holmes permitted the sterilization of supposed "mental defectives"—many speculated that his dissent, which is now seen by most historians and lawyers as the correct view, may have been motivated consciously or unconsciously by his deep Catholic faith. The Catholic church was inalterably opposed to sterilization of the mentally unfit, whereas the "progressive view," centered at Harvard University, strongly favored such "eugenic" procedures to "improve" the "race." The church was right and Harvard was wrong on that one, and it was a good thing that there was a religious Catholic on the high court to register a dissent to what we have now come to believe was an outrageous violation of human rights.

So the role of religion in judicial decision making is

complex, nuanced, and sometimes difficult to discuss. There is no sharp line between ideology and jurisprudence, but a line must be drawn nonetheless, especially when questioning a candidate for the Supreme Court.

Judge Amy Coney Barrett has now been nominated to the nation's highest court by President Trump. So the issue of religion is likely to come up at any confirmation hearing. It must be handled with delicacy and sensitivity to the Constitution's prohibition against religious tests, as well as with the respect we must all pay to people of faith.

Several years ago, a United States senator declared that he would never vote to confirm an atheist to the Supreme Court. Such a position is in direct conflict with the Constitution. But, because questions about religion are generally not asked of candidates, it is highly likely that several atheists and agnostics have served on the high court. Oliver Wendell Holmes publicly acknowledged his disbelief in religion and several other justices have privately acknowledged their lack of religious faith. One's religion is a private matter, but one's judicial philosophy is highly relevant in the confirmation process.

The confirmation process has become so politicalized, so personal, and often so unfair, that it is especially important to draw careful distinctions with regard to religious beliefs and observance. Let's hope the Senate handles this nomination better than they have handled other recent nominations.

The ranking Democrat, Senator Diane Feinstein, clearly mishandled the issue of her religion last time around. She offended Judge Barrett, many Catholics, and many Americans who believe in the constitutional prohibition against "religious tests" when she told Barrett that "the dogma lives loudly within you." Demeaning deeply held religious views by calling them "dogma" and focusing on them in a confirmation hearing is insulting to all Americans of faith. Moreover, it backfired as a tactic, turning an obscure judge into a folk hero among many religious Americans and increasing the chances she would be nominated to the high court by President Trump.

Having learned their lesson, the Democrats will have to be more cautious this time around. That doesn't mean they shouldn't ask Judge Barrett any questions about her moral and religious views and how they might impact her judicial decisions. Judge Barrett has herself opened the doors to questions about whether she will recuse herself from deciding cases in which the law may conflict with her moral and religious imperatives.

In 1998, she co-authored an article with Professor John Garvey of Notre Dame Law School on the issue of whether and when orthodox Catholic judges should be recused, or should recuse themselves, from sitting on cases in which their legal obligations may conflict with the mandatory obligations of their religion. The article focused on capital punishment, but its reasoning is applicable to abortion and other issues as well. That article was premised on the view that "We need to know whether judges are sometimes legally disqualified from hearing cases that their consciences would let them decide." Since Judge Barrett has written that "we need to know" this, she has certainly invited senators, and the public, to raise questions regarding this thorny issue.

The article concludes, quite correctly, that no Catholic judge should ever be recused simply because they are Catholic. That would amount to a "religious test," prohibited by the Constitution. Moreover, there are many Catholics who do not accept all the teachings or even mandates of their church. There are others—such as President John F. Kennedy, Governor Mario Cuomo, and Justice William Brennan—who have explicitly pledged to put their oath to support the Constitution and other secular law above their religious obligations.

The article specifically cites Governor Cuomo's defense of his decision to allow abortion in New York. Cuomo said that the "Catholics who hold office in a pluralistic democracy" must accord freedom to those who hold beliefs "different from specifically Catholic ones, sometimes contradictory to them," and that critics must have the right to engage in "conduct . . . which we would hold to be sinful." The article then quotes Justice Brennan's answer to a question put to him during his confirmation hearing, asking whether he could abide by his oath in cases where "matters of faith and morals got mixed up with matters of law and justice." Here is what Brennan said:

> Senator, [I took my] oath just as unreservedly as I know you did . . . And . . . there isn't any obligation of our faith superior to that. [In my service on the Court] what shall control me is the oath that I took to support the Constitution and laws of the United States and [I shall] so act upon the cases that come before me for decision that it is that oath and that alone which governs.

What is most significant is what Judge Barrett and her co-author then wrote about the positions taken by Governor Cuomo, Justice Brennan, and presumably President Kennedy:

> "We *do not* defend this position as the proper response for a Catholic judge to take with respect to abortion or the death penalty." (Emphasis added)

In other words, Judge Barrett has said that she is unwilling to commit to what other Catholic public officials have committed to: namely, to resolve conflicts between the law and the church in favor of the law.

Judge Barrett must now be asked, quite appropriately, whether she still stands by what she co-authored in 1998 when she was a law clerk who had recently graduated from law school. If not, what is her current position as an orthodox Catholic judge who may well be asked to sit on cases involving abortion and the death penalty? Will she recuse herself from all such cases? If not, what will be her criteria for recusal from some, but not all such cases?

What she wrote about recusal in capital punishment cases is even more relevant to abortion cases, because the views of the Catholic church are far more compulsory regarding the latter than the former. As she wrote:

> "The prohibitions against abortion and euthanasia (properly defined) are absolute; those against war and capital punishment are not."

The article ends with the following categorical imperative:

> "Judges cannot—nor should they try to—align our legal system with the Church's moral teaching whenever the two diverge. They should, however, conform their own behavior to the church's standard."

She should be asked what this means when the church's standard is at odds with what the Constitution or other laws demand.

Judge Barrett has not tried to hide the fact that her views with regard to the primacy of the Constitution over the teachings of the church appear to be different from those of other Catholics who have held high office in our pluralistic democracy. It is perfectly appropriate, therefore, to inquire about these apparent differences. But the questions and comments must be respectful of her religious views, and must give her a full opportunity to explain and justify her positions. She may point out, for example, that her constitutional views regarding abortion are not in conflict with the doctrines of her church, since under her view of the Constitution, there is no right to abortion despite the court's decision in *Roe v. Wade*, which she regards as erroneous. Nor would it be appropriate to try to psychoanalyze her to determine whether her constitutional views were unconsciously influenced by her religion. But it would be appropriate to press her with regard to her views on precedent: despite her legal opinion on the constitutionality of Roe v. Wade, would she feel bound as a justice to apply this nearly half-century-old precedent as a matter of law? And, if so, could she do so when it so clearly conflicts with the binding doctrines of her religion?

Judge Barrett has said that her religion commands her to believe—and act on the belief—that abortion is *always* immoral, under *all* circumstances: that the fetus has a *moral* right to life. She should be asked whether she believes that a fetus has a *constitutional* right to life. If it does, it might well follow that no state has the power to permit abortions under any circumstances. If that is her view—and she may very well say it is not—that would be a bridge too far for some Republican senators, who believe that the issue of abortion should be left to the states.

Judge Barrett is a serious intellectual and a serious Catholic, who has given considerable thought to possible conflicts between her faith and her obligations under our secular law. Senators and the public are entitled, indeed obligated, to provide her ample opportunity to elaborate on this important and relevant issue before she is confirmed for a seat on the Supreme Court, where she is likely to serve for decades and may be asked to cast many decisive votes in cases involving issues in which the governing secular law may conflict with the teachings of her church.

Chapter 7

The Role of Law Enforcement: Are We Prepared for Post-Election Violence?

We must prepare now for the possibility of violence following Election Day, especially in light of the contentious confirmation hearings that may well precede it, and the president's ambiguous answers during the first debate. If it turns out to be a close and contested election, extremists on both sides will use the controversy as an excuse to riot, loot, and attack. This will not be a repeat of the contested 2000 election, where the disputes were taken to court and ultimately resolved by the Supreme Court in a controversial 5-4 decision along partisan lines. The loser, Alan Gore, accepted the decision and told his followers to do the same. But this is not 2000, the candidates are not George Bush and Al Gore, and the mood of the nation is not what it was twenty years ago.

2020 is a very different and far more dangerous time. We are a more divided nation. Violence is in the air and has received a degree of legitimacy from people on both sides who should know better. We are not adequately prepared for the possibility of violent reactions to an election that may well seem unfair to people on one side or the other, depending on the outcome.

A perfect storm may be over the horizon: a pandemic which may get worse by early November; difficulties in voting—whether deliberate or simply a function of the pandemic; high unemployment, especially among the poor and lower-middle class; continued racial protests sometimes morphing into violence; massive wildfires in the west; rabid hatred of opposition candidates, fueled by the media taking sides and demonizing the opposition; criticism, defunding, lack of support, and physical attacks on police that disincentivize them from aggressively preventing and responding to violence; unwillingness of some DAs to prosecute violent protesters with whose goals they may agree; fear by some political leaders of alienating Black Lives Matter; weaponization of the justice system for partisan advantage; widespread distrust of governmental institution and leaders, as well as of the media; and many Americans in foul moods caused by isolation and other difficulties.

On top of these divisive factors, we may have a Supreme Court divided largely along partisan lines, with a vote deciding the election cast by a justice nominated by the winning litigant on the eve of the election.

These components of a perfect storm do not guarantee that there will be violence, but they surely increase the likelihood that violent extremists, and perhaps even people who, up to now, have not engaged in violence, may very well take to the streets instead of (or in addition to) the courts. Both sides are currently gearing up for anticipated court battles, as well they should. They must also be preparing for street battles, either before, during, or after the Supreme Court decides the case.

Preventing and responding to violence should be a bipartisan concern. Neither side ultimately benefits from lawlessness. Both benefit in the long run from stability and the rule of law. Only the most extreme elements on both sides, who want revolution rather than evolution, benefit from violence.

But there are those on both sides who subtly apply a different standard to violence, depending on its source. Some on the left "understand," if not justify, violent reactions to perceived racial injustice and police misconduct. Some on the right "understand," if not justify, violence against those who would tear down our nation, destroy statues of our founders, and attack our police. Both are wrong. There must be a single standard of condemnation of violence, regardless of its source or reason. Our constitution and laws provide peaceful remedies for wrongs, regardless of the source or reason. The role of violence is the antithesis of the rule of law.

Both parties and candidates should *now* announce that they condemn all violent reactions to the election, while supporting all appropriate legal remedies. The Justice Department should *now* be coordinating with state and local law enforcement officials. Attorney General Barr should *now* establish a bi-partisan task force to anticipate and prepare for any post-election violence. The key to preventing and responding to post-election violence is bi-partisan actions and words. If violence is encouraged—even subtly—by either side, it will persist and escalate.

We all have a stake in preventing violence, because its targets tend to be random and opportunistic. In recent riots and looting, the victims have included minority store owners and others who are merely in the wrong place at the wrong time. And when violence spreads, it provokes counterviolence. We are all potential victims.

The time to act is now, before the outcome of the election is known, and while we can still act against violence in a united bi-partisan manner. Once the election is over, and if it produces the kind of uncertain outcome reminiscent of 2000, it will be too late to present a united front against violence that will be perceived as supporting one side.

What is at stake is nothing less than the rule of law that benefits all Americans, regardless of party affiliation. We must preserve it against mob violence, whatever its source.

Conclusion

A recent article in *The New York Times*[1] quoted a source close to Joseph Biden as saying that the then-candidate "wants to restore the Court to its earlier place of respect," rather than its current status as an object of partisan intrigue and manipulation. The article also headlined the reality that the "Judicial wars started on Biden's watch" when he was a member and then-chairman of the Senate Judiciary Com-

---

1 Sept. 26, 2020 (5 Am ET).

mittee, which deals with judicial nominations. It quotes a speech Biden made to the Michigan Law School in 1991, in which he made two predictions: that a justice confirmed at that time would still "be making landmark decisions in the year 2020;" and that he, himself, will "be dead and gone, in all probability." He was right about the first: Justice Clarence Thomas, who was confirmed that year, is still very much participating in the making of landmark decisions, but Biden is still very much alive and in a position where he can possibly influence the future of the Supreme Court for many years.

As soon as President Trump announced the nomination of Judge Amy Coney Barrett—and said she could serve as long as "fifty years"—the Democrats started planning their response. Several proposals emerged. The most controversial is to "pack the Court" with additional justices if the Democrats were to win the presidency and the senate. All that is required to add additional justices is a simple majority of both houses and a non-veto by the president. Other proposals—such as term limits or mandatory retirement age for justices—would likely require constitutional amendments, which are nigh impossible without bi-partisan support.

The irony is that court packing would be the easiest

to accomplish but would be far more controversial than term limits or a mandatory retirement age.

Some Democrats, including perhaps Biden himself, would be reluctant to push for court packing. During the presidential primaries, before the death of Justice Ginsburg, Biden was pressed by some activists to embrace court packing. He rejected the idea, arguing that Democrats would "live to rue that day," implying that if Democrats voted to expand the court when they were in power, Republicans would do the same when they came to power. But then, after Justice Ginsburg died and the Republicans said they would fill the seat before the election, Biden vacillated, saying that "it's a legitimate question," but one he declined to answer. At the first presidential debate on September 29, 2020, Biden was asked a direct question about court packing. He again declined to answer, suggesting it was still on the table if the Democrats were to have the votes.

It was the fear of tit-for-tat politicization of the High Court that kept the filibuster and cloture safeguards in effect for so many years. And sure enough, when the Democrats ended these protections with regard to lower court judges, the Republicans soon ended them for Supreme Court Justices.

But now that the nomination and confirmation process has become a pure power play, with little regard for principle, precedent, or legitimate accusations of hypocrisy, all bets are off. Both parties are likely to do what they believe is best for their political and ideological interests, and let principles and precedents be damned. We are locked into a never-ending power struggle in which "when you have the votes, you can sort of do what you want. . . ."

So the question is, what will the Democrats do when they have votes, as they likely will sooner or later? Will they replicate the hardball tactics that they believe robbed them of at least one, perhaps two, seats on the Supreme Court? Will they try to do what Joseph Biden said he wanted to do: namely, restore the Supreme Court to its earlier place of respect? If so, how will they go about it?

There are several options. The easiest would be to reinstate the filibuster and cloture rules that permitted forty-one senators to block the nomination of a justice, but to use that anti-majoritarian rule only sparingly to prevent truly dangerous nominations. The reason that rule was changed was because it was abused for short-term partisan advantage by both parties. If both parties commit to using it only in extraordinary circumstances, it might serve a useful purpose.

But it is unlikely there would be agreement about its proper use. Consider the current nomination of Judge Amy Coney Barrett. She has all the professional qualifications to serve with distinction, but her confirmation as the swing vote just weeks before the presidential election outraged Democrats because of the Republican's refusal to even consider President Obama's nomination of a judge who was at least as qualified as she is. Moreover, her confirmation might endanger a woman's constitutional right to choose an abortion, Obamacare, and other Democratic agenda items. If the 3/5 rule were still in effect, it is likely that the Democratic leadership would deploy it against this highly qualified candidate for partisan and ideological reasons that would seem persuasive to many Democratic voters but utterly undemocratic and hypocritical to many Republicans.

We are so divided as a nation that it is impossible to come to agreement about almost anything involving the Supreme Court unless it involves issues with unknowable consequences for each party. Which brings us to term limits and mandatory retirement.

As an abstract matter, there may well be widespread agreement across party lines that justices of the Supreme Court should not serve for forty or more years and that nominating justices based on how young they are is not necessarily good for the court of the country. There may also be agreement that a fixed term of years—say, twenty—would be an improvement over the current constitutional criterion of "during good behavior." At the time the Constitution was drafted, life expectancies were considerably lower than they are today, and men who were appointed to serve on the High Court—and only men were appointed back then—tended to serve far shorter terms than many do today. There were, of course, some exceptions. Moreover, when nominations were less driven by ideological and partisan considerations, youth was less of a factor. Sixty-year-olds were frequently appointed and some defied the actuarial tables and served long terms, but most remained on the court in the range of twenty years.

As between term limits and a mandatory retirement age, I strongly prefer the former, because the latter would encourage the appointment of the youngest possible justices, while the former would make age less relevant.

Were a constitutional amendment to be proposed today—and one might well be proposed in the near future—to shorten the terms of sitting justices, it would not be considered on its abstract merits. Partisans would invoke my grandmother's criterion, calculate the immediate impact on the political balance of the Court and vote based on the answer to the question, "Is it good or bad for my party?"

Now that three relatively young justices have been appointed by President Trump, many Republicans— even some who favor term limitations for elected officials—will vote against these time limitations, unless they are made inapplicable to currently sitting justices.

The other proposal now being threatened by some Democrats is that if they were to control both the presidency and the senate, they should vote to pack the court with additional justices who would be nominated by their president. That could work in the short term to restore balance or return control to the liberal wing, but the longer-term implications would be that as soon as the Republicans took control of the presidency and senate, they would follow the Democrats' lead and once again expand the number of justices so that they could fill their seats with partisans. Since there is no constitutional limit to the number of justices, court packing by the Democrats would create an ever-expanding Court with diminishing credibility as a neutral and nonpartisan arbiter of justice.

So, it is unlikely, though not impossible, that we will see immediate structural changes to the Supreme Court, but the Democrats would not be without some weapons if and when they control the presidency and the senate. Through legislation and executive orders, they could do much to assure that women in need of abortion are able to secure them safely and effectively. They might be able to come up with a version of Obamacare that would pass constitutional muster, even by a conservative court.

Hamilton was correct when he pointed out that the greatest dangers to liberty come when the judiciary stands in "union with either of the other departments." The corollary to this wisdom is that when the president and the legislature serve as checks and balances against the excesses of the judiciary, we have less "to fear from the judiciary alone." That is the brilliance of our constitutional system of separation of power and checks and balances. This system may well be tested if an activist Supreme Court sets out to diminish the rights and liberties of women, minorities, and other vulnerable members of our society, but I believe it will pass the test.

An Israeli joke asks what is the difference between a pessimist and optimist? The answer: "A pessimist says things are so bad that they can't get any worse, while the optimist insists that they can." I'm that kind of optimist. I know that things can get worse, but I believe that our constitutional system and our love of liberty will maintain a proper balance.

DON'T PICK JUDGES
THE WAY WE DO!

In 1998, the British magazine Punch *asked me to compare the American and British systems for selecting judges. I used the article as an opportunity to write about judges, their powers, and the people selected to ascend the bench.*

As the British bench, bar, and public continue to debate the way judges are selected, I urge you, *please* do not look to my country for guidance. Britain and the United States are today separated not only by a common language but also by a common legal tradition. Yours is far too elitist. Ours is far too populist. There must surely be a happy medium somewhere between your white, male aristocracy of Oxbridge-educated former barristers and our politically correct amalgam of mediocre lawyers who happen to know a senator or a governor and happen to be of the race, gender, ethnicity, or political persuasion required to achieve the desired balance of the day.

Our judges are, of course, far more powerful and influential than are yours. Ours can strike down laws duly enacted by Congress, can enjoin the president from taking actions supported by a majority of our citizens, and can even require the state and federal governments to spend our tax dollars in ways of which we disapprove. Ours is the most powerful—some would say, meddlesome—judiciary in the world. Part of the reason is that we have a written constitution and the Bill of Rights. But so does Canada. Yet its courts are not nearly as influential as ours. We have a tradition of judicial activism that dates back to the time when Alexis de Tocqueville reported on the new republic and marveled at how every issue of significance eventually ended up in the American courts.

This extraordinary judicial power is necessarily a double-edged sword. Because the American courts have so much power over the political branches of our government—and over the daily lives of our citizens—it really matters to our citizens who sits on our courts. This explains, for example the remarkable confirmation battles we have been through over the nominations of judges such as Robert Bork, and the equally remarkable—if more disturbing—removal of judges such as Justice Rose Bird from her position as chief justice of California. The former was blocked because he was conservative; the latter was unseated because she was too liberal. It also explains why our Republican Senate is currently delaying the confirmation of dozens of Clinton nominees to the federal courts. Our judges are not perceived as nameless and faceless legal oracles who simply pronounce the law from under their homogenizing wigs. We know the names of our judges and we know their politics and predilections. And we darn well should—considering the reality that they may have as much influence over our daily lives as our elected executive and legislative branches.

Which brings me to the state court judges in our country, who are—in many states—*elected* to the judiciary. Yes, they actually run for office: they campaign, they raise money (mostly from lawyers who will appear before them), and they brag about how tough they will be on crime. The election of judges was part of the populism that swept our nation following its separation from Great Britain. We also elect most of our state prosecutors—a great stepping stone to higher office, as evidenced by the fact that President Bill Clinton, dozens of congressmen, and many governors were elected prosecutors before they went on to bigger and better things. In one state, Florida, they even vote for their public defenders. (Just imagine the campaign: candidate A boasts of his graduation from Harvard Law School and of his success rate in freeing accused murderers, robbers, and rapists, while candidate B proclaims his lack of qualifications and promises to lose most of his cases, thereby keeping the street safe from his clients—guess who would win.)

In sum, our system of picking judges in the worst in the Western world. In light of this sad reality, it is quite remarkable how many good judges have emerged from this wacky selection process. Some of the judges were picked by accident—the late, great justice William Brennan is a good example. He was picked because he was an urban, Irish-Catholic Democrat and President Dwight Eisenhower needed the votes of that particular constituency. (The conservative president who "accidentally" selected Brennan later regarded that

decision as the "worst mistake" of his presidency.)
Some judges were elected by defrauding the voters—
promising a lock-'em-up-and-throw-away-the-key ap-
proach and then breaking that promise by becoming
balanced jurists with a commitment to constitutional
principles. But occasional accidental excellence is not
a persuasive argument for perpetuating a system that
is inherently flawed. Our inherent flaw is our unwillingness to recognize that the judicial branch can serve
as a check and balance on the political branches only
if it is removed from partisan politics and shorn of its
hyper-populist input.

Does this mean that we should move toward
adopting your hyper-elitist system? No way! Your
system produces, on average, far more learned and
professionally respected judges—but at far too high a
cost. The cost of your flawed system is its perpetua-
tion of sexist and racist stereotypes and assumptions.
The small clique of elitists who select your wigged
Platonic guardians seem to believe—quite honestly—
that there is a white, male gene for intellect, integrity,
and professionalism. How else to explain the current
situation, in which of the ninety-three most highly
paid judges only seven are women and all are white?
No wonder that David Pannick, Q.C., described your

system as resembling a "pre-1965 Conservative leadership contest or a Papal conclave, rather than the
choice of lawmakers in a modern democracy." Others
have described it more simply as an "old boys' net-
work." Boys will pick boys, and boys from Oxford will
pick boys from Oxford.

Recently, a change was made under which the
position of high court judge will be "advertised" and
potential candidates can "apply" rather than wait to
be "tapped," as in some ancient fraternity ritual. But
this "reform" seems cosmetic, intended to head off
demands for more fundamental changes, such as the
proposal for a judicial appointment commission that
would include lay participants. Nonlawyers participating in the selection of judges frightens the established
bar as much as nonpriests selecting the pope would
scare the Catholic clergy. And there is good reason
for the concern: nonlawyers are more apt to subordinate professional qualifications to populist criteria.
Judges should be selected on the basis of merit and
professional qualifications, not on how well they pan-
der to popular taste. Accordingly, I do not favor lay
participation in the judicial selection process. That is
not an argument against a judicial commission; it is
only an argument for limiting the membership of such

a commission to members of the legal profession. But these lawyers can reflect the broadest array of professionals and not be limited to the old boys' club that currently whispers its approval of fellow Oxbridge barristers. The commission should include highly regarded academics, solicitors, and other members of the legal profession who are today excluded from the judicial selection process. It should also include younger lawyers, a change that would inevitably increase the number of women and ethnic minorities. This new blood would produce the names of qualified judicial candidates who are today unknown to the elitists who current pick judges. It would diversify the judiciary without compromising its quality.

Indeed, there is movement in some parts of the United States toward judicial selection commissions, but in our country these commissions are designed to ameliorate the populist and political influences on the judiciary rather than the elitist influences. In Massachusetts, for example, the governor appoints from a list prepared by such a commission; thus constraints are imposed on his ability to use the judiciary for patronage.

The virtue of a well-designed judicial selection commission is precisely that it is capable of ameliorating the extremes of both too much populism and too much elitism. Perhaps if both of our countries were to adopt such a system, we could narrow the separation between us and settle on that happy medium that does not sacrifice quality for diversity.

Appendix 2

The Recusal Statute

8 U.S. Code § 455.Disqualification of justice, judge, or magistrate judge

(a)

Any justice, judge, or magistrate judge of the United States shall disqualify himself in any proceeding in which his impartiality might reasonably be questioned.

(b)

He shall also disqualify himself in the following circumstances:

(1)

Where he has a personal bias or prejudice concerning a party, or personal knowledge of disputed evidentiary facts concerning the proceeding;

(2)

Where in private practice he served as lawyer in the matter in controversy, or a lawyer with whom he previously practiced law served during such association as a lawyer concerning the matter, or the judge or such lawyer has been a material witness concerning it;

(3)

Where he has served in governmental employment and in such capacity participated as counsel, adviser or material witness concerning the proceeding or expressed an opinion concerning the merits of the particular case in controversy;

(4)

He knows that he, individually or as a fiduciary, or his spouse or minor child residing in his household, has a financial interest in the subject matter in controversy or in a party to the proceeding, or any other interest that could be substantially affected by the outcome of the proceeding;

(5) He or his spouse, or a person within the third degree of relationship to either of them, or the spouse of such a person:

(i)

Is a party to the proceeding, or an officer, director, or trustee of a party;

(ii)

Is acting as a lawyer in the proceeding;

(iii)

Is known by the judge to have an interest that could be substantially affected by the outcome of the proceeding;

(iv)

Is to the judge's knowledge likely to be a material witness in the proceeding.

(c)

A judge should inform himself about his personal and fiduciary financial interests, and make a reasonable effort to inform himself about the personal financial interests of his spouse and minor children residing in his household.

(d)

For the purposes of this section the following words or phrases shall have the meaning indicated:

(1)

"proceeding" includes pretrial, trial, appellate review, or other stages of litigation;

(2)

the degree of relationship is calculated according to the civil law system;

(3)

"fiduciary" includes such relationships as executor, administrator, trustee, and guardian;

(4)

"financial interest" means ownership of a legal or equitable interest, however small, or a relationship as director, adviser, or other active participant in the affairs of a party, except that:

(i)

Ownership in a mutual or common investment fund that holds securities is not a "financial interest" in such securities unless the judge participates in the management of the fund;

(ii)

An office in an educational, religious, charitable, fraternal, or civic organization is not a "financial interest" in securities held by the organization;

(iii)

The proprietary interest of a policyholder in a mutual

insurance company, of a depositor in a mutual savings association, or a similar proprietary interest, is a "financial interest" in the organization only if the outcome of the proceeding could substantially affect the value of the interest;

(iv)

Ownership of government securities is a "financial interest" in the issuer only if the outcome of the proceeding could substantially affect the value of the securities.

(e)

No justice, judge, or magistrate judge shall accept from the parties to the proceeding a waiver of any ground for disqualification enumerated in subsection (b). Where the ground for disqualification arises only under subsection (a), waiver may be accepted provided it is preceded by a full disclosure on the record of the basis for disqualification.

(f)

Notwithstanding the preceding provisions of this section, if any justice, judge, magistrate judge, or bankruptcy judge to whom a matter has been assigned would be disqualified, after substantial judicial time has been devoted to the matter, because of the appearance or discovery, after the matter was assigned to him or her, that he or she individually or as a fiduciary, or his or her spouse or minor child residing in his or her household, has a financial interest in a party (other than an interest that could be substantially affected by the outcome), disqualification is not required if the justice, judge, magistrate judge, bankruptcy judge, spouse or minor child, as the case may be, divests himself or herself of the interest that provides the grounds for the disqualification.

(June 25, 1948, ch. 646, 62 Stat. 908; Pub. L. 93–512, § 1, Dec. 5, 1974, 88 Stat. 1609; Pub. L. 95–598, title II, § 214(a), (b), Nov. 6, 1978, 92 Stat. 2661; Pub. L. 100–702, title X, § 1007, Nov. 19, 1988, 102 Stat. 4667; Pub. L. 101–650, title III, § 321, Dec. 1, 1990, 104 Stat. 5117.)

Historical and Revision Notes

Based on title 28, U.S.C., 1940 ed., § 24 (Mar. 3, 1911, ch. 231, § 20, 36 Stat. 1090).

Section 24 of title 28, U.S.C., 1940 ed., applied only to district judges. The revised section is made applicable to all justices and judges of the United States.

The phrase "in which he has a substantial interest" was substituted for "concerned in interest in any suit."

The provision of section 24 of title 28, U.S.C., 1940 ed., as to giving notice of disqualification to the "senior circuit judge," and words "and thereupon such proceedings shall be had as are provided in sections 17 and 18 of this title," were omitted as unnecessary and covered by section 291 et seq. of this title relating to designation and assignment of judges. Such provision is not made by statute in case of disqualification or incapacity, for other cause. See sections 140, 143, and 144 of this title. If a judge or clerk of court is remiss in failing to notify the chief judge of the district or circuit, the judicial council of the circuit has ample power under section 332 of this title to apply a remedy.

Relationship to a party's attorney is included in the revised section as a basis of disqualification in conformity with the views of judges cognizant of the grave possibility of undesirable consequences resulting from a less inclusive rule.

Changes were made in phraseology.

Amendments

1988—Subsec. (f). Pub. L. 100–702 added subsec. (f).

1978—Pub. L. 95–598 struck out references to referees in bankruptcy in section catchline and in subsecs. (a) and (e).

1974—Pub. L. 93–512 substituted "Disqualification of justice, judge, magistrate, or referee in bankruptcy" for "Interest of justice or judge" in section catchline, reorganized structure of provisions, and expanded applicability to include magistrates and referees in bankruptcy and grounds for which disqualification may be based, and inserted provisions relating to waiver of disqualification.

Change of Name

Words "magistrate judge" substituted for "magistrate" in section catchline and wherever appearing in subsecs. (a), (e), and (f) pursuant to section 321 of Pub. L. 101–650, set out as a note under section 631 of this title.

Effective Date of 1978 Amendment

Amendment by Pub. L. 95–598 effective Oct. 1, 1979, see section 402(c) of Pub. L. 95–598, set out as an

Effective Date note preceding section 101 of Title 11, Bankruptcy. For procedures relating to Bankruptcy matters during transition period see note preceding section 151 of this title.

Effective Date of 1974 Amendment

Pub. L. 93–512, § 3, Dec. 5, 1974, 88 Stat. 1610, provided that:

"This Act [amending this section] shall not apply to the trial of any proceeding commenced prior to the date of this Act [Dec. 5, 1974], nor to appellate review of any proceeding which was fully submitted to the reviewing court prior to the date of this Act."

Acknowledgments

This short book could not have been published so quickly without the help of my assistant, Maura Kelley. Aaron Voloj proofread it and made good suggestions, as did other friends. As always, my wife Carolyn inspired me, while not always agreeing with my arguments. I tested my ideas with my sons, Elon and Jamin, my daughter Ella, and her fiancé Dave, who also disagreed with some of my points, but never in a disagreeable way.

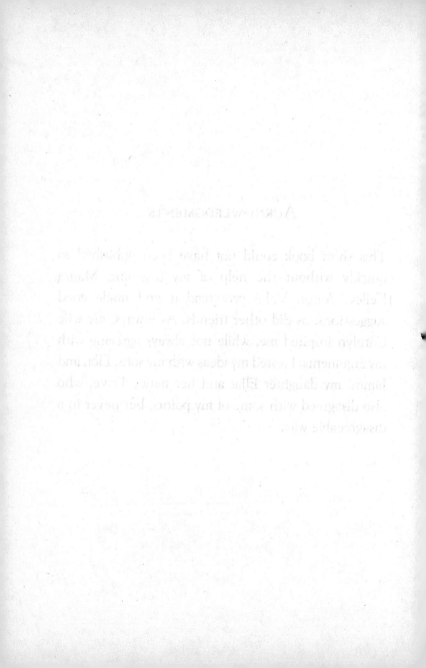